753

ADAMASTOR

ADAMASTOR

POEMS

BY

ROY CAMPBELL

Author of "The Flaming Terrapin"

LINCOLN MAC VEAGH
THE DIAL PRESS
NEW YORK · MCMXXXI

MANUFACTURED IN THE UNITED STATES OF AMERICA
BY THE VAIL-BALLOU PRESS, INC., BINGHAMTON, N. Y.

NOTE

Some of these poems have appeared in *The Enemy*, *Commerce*, *The Calendar of Modern Letters*, *Life and Letters*, *Voorslag*, *The New Statesman*, *The Nation and Athenaeum*, *The Cape Times* and *The South African Nation*.

DEDICATION

(TO MARY CAMPBELL)

When in dead lands where men like brutish herds
Rush to and fro by aimless frenzies borne,
Firing a golden fusillade of words,
Lashing his laughter like a knotted scourge,
A poet of his own disdain is born
And dares among the rabble to emerge—

His humble kindred sicken to behold
This monstrous changeling whom they schooled in
    vain,
Who brings no increase to their hoard of gold,
Who lives by sterner laws than they have known
And worships, even where their idols reign,
A god superbly stronger than their own.

Accursèd in the temples of the Pagan
His evil fame is borne on every wind:
His name is thundered by the priests of Dagon,
And all Philistia whispers with the plot
To shear his sleeping head, his eyes to blind,
And chain his ankle to a trundling shot:

For That which o'er their cities far-espied
Decreed his spirit like a torch to shine,
Has fired him with the peacock's flaunting pride

Who still would fan his embers to a blaze
Though it were but to startle grunting swine
Or herds of sleepy cattle to amaze.

Insulting their dull sense with gorgeous dyes,
The matador of truth, he trails his scorn
Before their lowered horns and bloodshot eyes—
For never can their stubborn necks be tamed
Until they know how laughter must be borne
And learn to look on beauty unashamed.

Even this were victory, though by his foes
On every side with plunging hoofs beset,
Reeling at last beneath their leaden blows,
Behind some heap of filth he should be flung
Whereon the spider spreads his dusty net
And the cold viper hatches out her young.

But when the Muse or some as lovely sprite,
Friend, lover, wife, in such a form as thine,
Thrilling a mortal frame with half her light
And choosing for her guise such eyes and hair
As scarcely veil the subterfuge divine,
Descends with him his lonely fight to share—

He knows his gods have watched him from afar,
And he may take her beauty for a sign
That victory attends him as a star,
Shaped like a Valkyrie for his delight

In lovely changes through the day to shine
And be the glory of the long blue night.

When my spent heart had drummed its own retreat,
You rallied the red squadron of my dreams
Turning the crimson rout of their defeat
Into a white assault of seraphim
Invincibly arrayed with flashing beams
Against a night of spectres foul and grim.

Sweet sister, through all earthly treasons true,
My life has been the enemy of slumber:
Bleak are the waves that lash it, but for you
And your clear faith, I am a locked lagoon
That circles with its jagged reef of thunder
The calm blue mirror of the stars and moon.

January, 1929

CONTENTS

SATIRICAL FRAGMENTS

EARLY POEMS

DEDICATED TO
C. J. SIBBETT

THE THEOLOGY OF BONGWI, THE BABOON

This is the wisdom of the Ape
    Who yelps beneath the Moon—
'Tis God who made me in His shape,
    He is a Great Baboon.
'Tis He who tilts the moon askew
    And fans the forest trees,
The heavens which are broad and blue
    Provide him his trapeze,
He swings with tail divinely bent
    Around those azure bars
And munches to his Soul's content
    The kernels of the stars;
And when I die, his loving care
    Will raise me from the sod
To learn the perfect Mischief there,
    The Nimbleness of God.

HIALMAR

The firing ceased and like a wounded foe
The day bled out in crimson: wild and high
A far hyena sent his voice of woe
Tingling in faint hysteria through the sky.

Thick lay the fatal harvest of the fight
In the grey twilight when the newly-dead
Collect those brindled scavengers of night
Whose bloodshot eyes must candle them to bed.

The dead slept on: but one among them rose
Out of his trance, and turned a patient eye
To where like cankers in a burning rose,
Out of the fading scarlet of the sky,

Great birds, descending, settled on the stones:
He knew their errand and he knew how soon
The wolf must make a pulpit of his bones
To skirl his shrill hosannas to the moon.

Great adjutants came wheeling from the hills,
And chaplain crows with smug, self-righteous face,
And vultures bald and red about the gills
As any hearty colonel at the base.

All creatures that grow fat on beauty's wreck,
They ranged themselves expectant round the kill,

And like a shrivelled arm each raw, red neck
Lifted the rusty dagger of its bill.

Then to the largest of that bony tribe
"O merry bird," he shouted, "work your will,
I offer my clean body as a bribe
That when upon its flesh you've gorged your fill,

"You'll take my heart and bear it in your beak
To where my sweetheart combs her yellow hair
Beside the Vaal: and if she bids you speak
Tell her you come to represent me there.

"Flounce out your feathers in their sleekest trim,
Affect the brooding softness of the dove—
Yea, smile, thou skeleton so foul and grim,
As fits the bland ambassador of love!

"And tell her, when the nights are wearing late
And the grey moonlight smoulders on her hair,
To brood no more upon her ghostly mate
Nor on the phantom children she would bear.

"Tell her I fought as blindly as the rest,
That none of them had wronged me whom I killed,
And she may seek within some other breast
The promise that I leave her unfulfilled.

"I should have been too tired for love or mirth
Stung as I am, and sickened by the truth—
Old men have hunted beauty from the earth
Over the broken bodies of our youth!"

MAZEPPA

Helpless, condemned, yet still for mercy croaking
Like a trussed rooster swinging by the claws,
They hoisted him: they racked his joints asunder;
They lashed his belly to a thing of thunder—
A tameless brute, with hate and terror smoking,
That never felt the bit between its jaws.

So when his last vain struggle had subsided,
His gleeful butchers wearied of the fun:
Looping the knots about his thighs and back,
With lewd guffaws they heard his sinews crack,
And laughed to see his lips with foam divided,
His eyes too glazed with blood to know the sun.

A whip cracked, they were gone: alone they followed
The endless plain: the long day volleyed past
With only the white clouds above them speeding
And the grey steppe into itself receding,
Where each horizon, by a vaster swallowed,
Repeated but the bareness of the last.

Out of his trance he wakened: on they flew:
The blood ran thumping down into his brain:
With skull a-dangle, facing to the sky
That like a great black wind went howling by,
Foaming, he strove to gnash the tethers through
That screwed his flesh into a knot of pain.

7

To him the earth and sky were drunken things—
Bucked from his senses, jolted to and fro,
He only saw them reeling hugely past,
As sees a sailor soaring at the mast,
Who retches as his sickening orbit swings
The sea above him and the sky below.

Into his swelling veins and open scars
The python cords bit deeper than before,
And the great beast, to feel their sharpened sting,
Looping his body in a thundrous sling
As if to jolt his burden to the stars,
Recoiled, and reared, and plunged ahead once more.

Three days had passed, yet could not check nor tire
That cyclone whirling in its spire of sand:
Charged with resounding cordite, as they broke
In sudden flashes through the flying smoke,
The fusillading hoofs in rapid fire
Rumbled a dreary volley through the land.

Now the dark sky with gathering ravens hums:
And vultures, swooping down on his despair,
Struck at the loose and lolling head whereunder
The flying coffin sped, the hearse of thunder
Whose hoof-beats with the roll of muffled drums
Led on the black processions of the air.

The fourth sun saw the great black wings descending
Where crashed in blood and spume the charger lay:
From the snapped cords a shapeless bundle falls—
Scarce human now, like a cut worm he crawls
Still with a shattered arm his face defending
As inch by inch he drags himself away.

Who'd give a penny for that strip of leather?
Go, set him flapping in a field of wheat,
Or take him as a pull-through for your gun,
Or hang him up to kipper in the sun,
Or leave him here, a strop to hone the weather
And whet the edges of the wind and sleet.

Who on that brow foresees the gems aglow?
Who, in that shrivelled hand, the sword that swings
Wide as a moonbeam through the farthest regions,
To crop the blood-red harvest of the legions,
Making amends to every cheated crow
And feasting vultures on the fat of kings?

This is that Tartar prince, superbly pearled,
Whose glory soon on every wind shall fly,
Whose arm shall wheel the nations into battle,
Whose warcry, rounding up the tribes like cattle,
Shall hurl his cossacks rumbling through the world
As thunder hurls the hail-storm through the sky.

And so it is whenever some new god,
Boastful, and young, and avid of renown,
Would make his presence known upon the earth—
Choosing some wretch from those of mortal birth,
He takes his body like a helpless clod
And on the croup of genius straps it down.

With unseen hand he knots the cord of pain,
Unseen the wingèd courser strains for flight:
He leads it forth into some peopled space
Where the dull eyes of those who throng the place
See not the wings that wave, the thews that strain,
But only mark the victim of their might.

Left for the passing rabble to admire,
He fights for breath, he chokes, and rolls his eyes:
They mime his agonies with loud guffaws,
They pelt him from the place with muddy paws,
Nor do they hear the sudden snort of fire
To which the tether snaps, the great wings rise. . . .

Vertiginously through the heavens rearing,
Plunging through chasms of eternal pain,
Splendours and horrors open on his view,
And wingèd fiends like fiercer kites pursue,
With hateful patience at his side careering,
To hook their claws of iron on his brain.

Beyond the limits of the world we know
He sees what none have ever dared to dream—
Glories that have no name in mortal breath
And terrors starker than the self of death,
Heavens of song, and hells of endless woe—
And Solitude, above all else supreme.

Out of his pain, perhaps, some god-like thing
Is born. A god has touched him, though with whips:
We only know that, hooted from our walls,
He hurtles on his way, he reels, he falls,
And staggers up to find himself a king
With truth a silver trumpet at his lips.

A VELD ECLOGUE: THE PIONEERS

On the bare veld where nothing ever grows
Save beards and nails and blisters on the nose,
Johnny and Piet, two simple shepherds, lay
Watching their flock grow thinner every day—
Their one joint Nanny-goat, poor trustful thing,
That by the fence had waited since last spring
Lest any of the stakes that there were stuck
Should sprout a withered leaf for her to suck.
Rough was the labour of those hardy swains,
Sometimes they lay and waited for the rains,
Sometimes with busy twigs they switched the flies
Or paused to damn a passing nigger's eyes:
Sometimes, as now, they peeled them off their hose
And hacked the jiggers from their gnarly toes.
At times they lay and watched their blisters heal,
At others, sweated forth a scanty meal
Prone on their backs between their Nanny's shins—
After the manner of the Roman twins.
What wonder then, at such a flurry kept,
That sometimes—oftenest of all—they slept?
Yet for all that their simple hearts were gay,
And often would they trill the rustic lay,
For though the times were hard they could not bilk
Their brains of nonsense or their guts of milk;
And loud upon the hills with merry clang
The grand old saga of "Ferreira" rang,
Till the Baboons upon the topmost krans

12

Would leap for joy, career into a dance,
And all their Simian dignity forgot
Would hold a sort of Nagmaal on the spot,
Or, if to such comparisons we stoop—
A special rally of the Empire Group.
Think not that I on racial questions touch
For one was Durban-born, the other Dutch.
I draw no line between them: for the two
Despise each other, and with reason too!
But, in this case, they both forgave the sin,
Each loved the other as a very twin—
One touch of tar-brush makes the whole world kin.
That they were true-bred children of the veld
It could as easily be seen as smelt,
For clumsier horsemen never sat astride,
Worse shots about their hunting never lied—
Though Piet once laid a lioness out straight,
I must confess—through aiming at its mate;
And Johnny, though he stalked extremely well,
Even against the wind the game could smell:
Even a pole-cat wheezing with catarrh
Could have discerned his presence from afar.
One knew them at a glance for Pioneers
Though Piet, but two years since, had washed his ears:
Their musty jackets and moth-eaten hair
Showed them for children of the Open Air;
Besides red tufts, there shone upon their faces
That "nameless something" which Bolitho traces
To gazing out across the "open spaces",

As if the sharpest Taakhaar that he knows
Can see an inch beyond his own red nose,
As if the meanest cockney in existence
Can't see the sky at a far greater distance
With sun and moon and stars to blink his eyes on
Much farther off than any fenced horizon,
And Sirius and Aldebaran, forsooth,
As far away as he is from the truth.
But "nameless somethings" and "unbounded spaces"
Are still the heritage of "younger races"—
At least our novelists will have it so,
And, reader, who are we to tell them, "No!"
We, who have never heard the "call," or felt
The witching whatdyecallum of the veld.
As for that "nameless something," it was there
Plain as the grime upon their ragged hair—
Bolitho calls it an "inspired alertness"
And so it seemed (in spite of their inertness)—
A worried look, as if they half-expected
Something to happen, or half-recollected
Anything having happened there at all
Since old Oom Jaapie's heifer calved last fall.
As for the "boundless spaces"—wild and free
They stretched around as far as eye could see,
Which, though not very far, was yet enough
To show a tree, four houses, and a bluff.
Geographers, who say the world's a sphere,
Are either ignorant, or mazed with beer,
Or liars—or have never read two pages

Of any of our novelists or sages
Who tell us plainly that the world's more wide
On the colonial than the other side,
That states and kingdoms are less vast and grand
Than ranches, farms and mealie-planted land,
And that wherever on the world's bald head
A province or protectorate is spread
The place straightway to vast proportions jumps
As with the goitre or a dose of mumps—
So that in shape our cosmos should compare
Less with an apple than a warty pear.
For all our scenery's in grander style
And there are far more furlongs to the mile
In Africa than Europe—though, no doubt
None but colonials have found this out.
For though our Drakensberg's most lofty scalps
Would scarcely reach the waist-line of the Alps,
Though Winterberg, beside the Pyrenees,
Would scarcely reach on tip-toe to their knees,
Nobody can deny that our hills rise
Far more majestically—for their size!
I mean that there is something grander, yes,
About the veld, than I can well express,
Something more vast—perhaps I don't mean that—
Something more round, and square, and steep, and
      flat—
No, well perhaps it's not quite that I mean
But something, rather, half-way in between,
Something more "nameless"— That's the very word!

Something that can't be felt, or seen, or heard,
Or even thought—a kind of mental mist
That doesn't either matter or exist
But without which it would go very hard
With many a local novelist and bard—
Being the only trick they've ever done,
To bring in local colour where there's none:
And if I introduce the system too,
Blame only the traditions I pursue.

We left our shepherds in their open spaces
Sunning the "nameless somethings" on their faces,
And also (but that's neither here nor there)
Scratching the "nameless somethings" in their hair.
And there I'll leave them to complete my rhyme
In conversation learned and sublime:—

PIET

That you're a poet, Johnny, you declare
Both in your verses and your length of hair,
And sure, why not? we've prophets in the land
Fit with the best of Israel's line to stand—
For Balaam's donkey only made him curse
But Totius' Ox inspired him into verse,
And I have often thought some work of note
Could well be written round our faithful goat;
And heroes of Thermopylae were writers
And sculptors too—in spite of being fighters—

The heroes of Bull-hoek and Bondleswaart
Should not be backward in the field of art.
Come—the Jew's-harp!—I'll thrum it while you
    sing,
Arise, and soar on music's golden wing!

JOHNNY

A simple goat was in her owners blest,
They milked her twice a day, then let her rest:
No wrangling rose between them—all was fair—
Which owned the head, or tail, they did not care:
Think not that I on racial questions touch
For one was British and the other Dutch.

So Johnny sang. His song was brief and true—
Had Creswell, Smuts or Hertzog half his nous,
There would be far more goats on the Karroo
And far less in the Senate and the House.

BUFFEL'S KOP

(OLIVE SCHREINER'S GRAVE)

In after times when strength or courage fail,
May I recall this lonely hour: the gloom
Moving one way: all heaven in the gale
Roaring: and high above the insulted tomb
An eagle anchored on full spread of sail
That from its wings let fall a silver plume.

GEORGIAN SPRING

Who does not love the spring deserves no lovers—
For peaches bloom in Georgia in the spring,
New quarterlies relume their yellow covers,
Anthologies on every bookshelf sing.
The publishers put on their best apparel
To sell the public everything it wants—
A thousand meek soprano voices carol
The loves of homosexuals or plants.
Now let the Old Cow perish, for the tune
Would turn the fatted calf to bully beef:
We know, we know, that "silver is the Moon",
That "skies are blue" was always our belief:
That "grass is green" there can be no denying,
That titled whores in love can be forgot—
All who have heard poor Georgiana sighing
Would think it more surprising were they not:
As for the streams, why, any carp or tench
Could tell you that they "sparkle on their way".
Now for the millionth time the "country wench"
Has lost her reputation "in the hay".
But still the air is full of happy voices,
All bloody: but no matter, let them sing!
For who would frown when all the world rejoices,
And who would contradict when, in the spring,
The English Muse her annual theme rehearses
To tell us birds are singing in the sky?
Only the poet slams the door and curses,
And all the little sparrows wonder why!

ST. PETER OF THE THREE CANALS

(THE FISHER'S PRAYER)

High in his niche above the town,
The three canals with garbage brown,
The rolling waves, and windy dunes—
An old green idol, thunder-scarred,
On whom the spray has crusted hard,
A shell-backed saint, whom time maroons

High stranded on the Rock of Ages,
Of all the ocean-gods and mages
The last surviving Robinson—
Saint Peter-Neptune fronts the wind,
In whose Protean rôle combined
All deities and creeds are One.

For when the Three-in-One grow thrifty,
Saint Peter, he is One in Fifty,
Saint Peter, he is All in All!
And I have heard the fishers tell
How when from forth the jaws of hell
No other saint would heed their call,

Doomed wretches at the swamping rowlocks
Have seen a saintly Castor-Pollux,
Walking the waves, a burning wraith,
Speed to their aid with strides that quicken
As light as Mother Carey's chicken
Foot-webbed with Mercy and with Faith.

Oh, strong is he when winds are strident
To tame the water with his trident,
And bold is he when thunders fly,
And swift—outspeeding as he runs
The corposants of Leda's sons—
To heed the sailor's drowning cry.

By his high tower of creviced rock
The time is always twelve o'clock—
High tower, high time to save our souls!
And hark! his husky bells are calling
By faith and ivy kept from falling
When the night-long mistral rolls.

Deriding Newton, firm and fast,
His crazy tower withstands the blast
A shining miracle to prove—
For all can see, when winds are great,
It needs more faith to keep him straight
Than would a range of mountains move.

Around him float on airy sculls
Bright angels in the form of gulls
His seaward messages to go:
Deep in his bosom nest the doves
In token of seraphic loves,
To keep his garments—white as snow.

Archbishop of the deep-sea Tritons,
When round his head the glory lightens,
Mitred by the moon with flame,
Safe in the harbour that he guards
The masts, adoring, lift their yards
The signal of the cross to frame.

Among the clouds his feet are set,
And in his hands the spangled net
Where souls of men, as small red fish,
Smoked with spindrift, soused in spray,
And salted till the Judgment Day,
Await the great Millennial Dish.

Amphibious saint, crustacean idol,
At once celestial and tidal,
To his bland creed all doubt atones—
Where Dagon weds with Mother Carey,
Jehovah woos a Mermaid Mary,
And Thetis sins with Davey Jones.

Arch-patriarch of Navigation,
He bears the lifebuoy of Salvation
To souls that flounder in the lurch:
With God he walks the azure decks,
Great Quartermaster-Pontifex
Whose vessel is the Holy Church.

Her sails are swelled with hymns, her spars
Are pulleyed with the moon and stars
From which depend, a hardy gang,
Her crew of human fears and hopes—
And metaphysics are the ropes
By which those desperadoes hang.

Her ropes with love and faith are spliced,
Her compass is the Cross of Christ,
Pointing the quarters of the world,
And her auxiliary steam
The vapour of the prophet's dream
To waft her when the winds are furled.

With track of fire she cleaves the distance,
To genuflexions of her pistons
The rapture of the turbine rolls:
Her stokehold is the deep Avernus
Where Satan feeds the roaring furnace
And sinners are the burning coals. . . .

O Captain of the Saint-filled Ark,
Ere loaded to the Plimsoll mark
Your saintly cargo put to sea,
And we attend the Great Inspection,
The Roll-call of the Resurrection,
The pay-day of Eternity—

23

Remember in your high promotion
How once, poor flotsam of the Ocean,
You followed such a trade as mine.
The winter nights, have you forgotten,
When hauling on a seine as rotten
You cracked your knuckles on the line?

Have you forgot the cramp that clinches
Your shoulder, turning at the winches—
And not a mullet in the mesh?
Have you forgotten Galilee—
The night you floundered in the sea
Because your faith was in your flesh?

Be with me, then, when nights are lone
And from the pampas of the Rhone,
Thrilling with sleet, the great guns blow,
When the black mistral roars avenging
Increase the horse-power of my engine,
Hallow my petrol ere I go!

SOLO AND CHORUS FROM "THE CONQUISTADOR"

Solo.   Come, we are hungry; bake us bread,
        Great sun: you torrents, grind the flour:
        Nuggets of gold and rubies red,
        Sprinkle the buns that we devour:
        Bring the great rocks from ovens dark,
        Digest the grim diluvial cakes—
        The old ships-biscuits of the Ark,
        The cookery of seas and lakes.

Chorus.   *O bake for us the red, the blue,*
           The boulders of the broad Karroo.

Solo.   The sun eats mud and fire: in sleep
        We hanker for such foods, alas,
        Our thoughts like flocks of springbok sweep
        The vastitudes of bitter grass:
        With rasp of roots pasture creaks,
        Tugging harsh stems our tongues are curled—
        Come quit these pastures for the peaks
        Before we devastate the world.

Chorus.   *Not while so green a salad fills*
           The blue bowl of the circling hills.

Solo.   Up there, the sun on grills of gold
        Fries the red clouds for you and me,
        The huge cooks of the whirlwind scold
        And on their spits revolve the free,

25

Roast phœnixes, for all who ask,
With battered breast and frizzled legs—
Then leave your dull prosaic task
And feast upon the angels' eggs!
Chorus.   *Our farms are ringed with peaceful trees*
    Where fatter poultry roost than these.

Solo.   The frisky gnus that gallop there
And kick their heels into the sky,
Singed by the stars, with tails aflare,
Stampede across the mountains high:
They'll fire the grass, they'll char the roots
And bring a famine on the herds—
We strove to pacify the brutes,
It was too late to bandy words.
Chorus.   *No more these rolling plains, O chief,*
    Shall thunder under tons of beef.

Solo.   O sound the sanguinary drums
As to the North our rule extends,
And if you do not trust your guns,
Diplomacy will gain your ends:
Recall the fights your fathers won
Against such odds, in such a fix—
The rattle of the maxim-gun
Against the clattering of sticks.
Chorus.   *When the hurly-burly's done*
    Let smoke and thunder quench the sun.

Solo.   Then fly, my wolf-pack, on before,
Swift in your pilgrimage of hope,
And I shall follow on your spoor
To kiss the bunions of the Pope:
A thousand priests, behind our thunder,
Shall follow with the crow and kite,
To cure the wounds of those we plunder
With words of mercy, hope, and light!

ROUNDING THE CAPE

The low sun whitens on the flying squalls,
Against the cliffs the long grey surge is rolled
Where Adamastor from his marble halls
Threatens the sons of Lusus as of old.

Faint on the glare uptowers the dauntless form,
Into whose shade abysmal as we draw,
Down on our decks, from far above the storm,
Grin the stark ridges of his broken jaw.

Across his back, unheeded, we have broken
Whole forests: heedless of the blood we've spilled,
In thunder still his prophecies are spoken,
In silence, by the centuries, fulfilled.

Farewell, terrific shade! though I go free
Still of the powers of darkness art thou Lord:
I watch the phantom sinking in the sea
Of all that I have hated or adored.

The prow glides smoothly on through seas quiescent:
But where the last point sinks into the deep,
The land lies dark beneath the rising crescent,
And Night, the Negro, murmurs in his sleep.

ADAMASTOR

THE MAKING OF A POET

In every herd there is some restive steer
Who leaps the cows and heads each hot stampede,
Till the old bulls unite in jealous fear
To hunt him from the pastures where they feed.

Lost in the night he hears the jungles crash
And desperately, lest his courage fail,
Across his hollow flanks with sounding lash
Scourges the heavy whipcord of his tail.

Far from the phalanxes of horns that ward
The sleeping herds he keeps the wolf at bay,
At nightfall by the slinking leopard spoored,
And goaded by the fly-swarm through the day.

A SONG FOR THE PEOPLE

I sing the people; shall the Muse deny
The weak, the blind, the humble and the lame
Who have no purpose save to multiply,
Who have no will save all to be the same:
I sing the people as I watch, untamed,
Its aimless pomps and generations roll—
A monster whom the drunken gods have maimed
And set upon a road that has no goal.

How fiercely callous Nature plies her whips
When that tame hydra on the light uprears
Huge buttock-faces slashed with flabby lips,
Gouged into eyes, and tortured into ears.
A shapeless mass to any rhythm worked,
See how its legs to raucous music stir
As if some string of sausages were jerked,
And tugged, and worried by a snarling cur!

Do they too have their loves, and with these clods
Of bodies do they dare in their abodes
To parody our dalliance, or the gods',
By coupling in the chilly sport of toads?
Do they too feel and hate—under our wheels
Could they be crushed the deeper in the slime
When forth we ride elate with bloody heels,
Or jingle in the silver spurs of rhyme?

32

Funnelled with roaring mouths that gorp like cod
And spit the bitten ends of thick cigars,
This is the beast that dares to praise its god
Under the calm derision of the stars!
When from the lonely beacons that we tend
We gaze far down across the nameless flats,
Where the dark road of progress without end .
Is cobbled with a line of bowler hats,

Searching the lampless horror of that fen,
We think of those whose pens or swords have made
Steep ladders of the broken bones of men
To climb above its everlasting shade:
Of men whose scorn has turned them into gods,
Christs, tyrants, martyrs, who in blood or fire
Drove their clean furrows through these broken clods
Yet raised no harvest from such barren mire.

In the cold hour when poets light their tapers
And the tall Muse glides naked to the door,
When by its loves, its drinks, its evening papers,
All Babel has been lulled into a snore,
The pious poet in that silence hears
Like some pure hymn uplifting his desires
How Nero's fiddle shrills across the years
And to its music leap the dancing fires—

And the great Master of the radiant spheres
Turns from the sleeping multitudes in scorn

To where he sees our lonely flames and hears,
As when before him sang the sons of morn,
Down the far ages ringing lofty chimes,
High o'er the prayers of that huge carrion soul,
Our sacrifices, miracles, and crimes,
Up to the Throne their sounding anthems roll.

THE SERF

His naked skin clothed in the torrid mist
That puffs in smoke around the patient hooves,
The ploughman drives, a slow somnambulist,
And through the green his crimson furrow grooves.
His heart, more deeply than he wounds the plain,
Long by the rasping share of insult torn,
Red clod, to which the war-cry once was rain
And tribal spears the fatal sheaves of corn,
Lies fallow now. But as the turf divides
I see in the slow progress of his strides
Over the toppled clods and falling flowers,
The timeless, surly patience of the serf
That moves the nearest to the naked earth
And ploughs down palaces, and thrones, and towers.

THE ZULU GIRL

When in the sun the hot red acres smoulder,
Down where the sweating gang its labour plies,
A girl flings down her hoe, and from her shoulder
Unslings her child tormented by the flies.

She takes him to a ring of shadow pooled
By thorn-trees: purpled with the blood of ticks,
While her sharp nails, in slow caresses ruled,
Prowl through his hair with sharp electric clicks,

His sleepy mouth, plugged by the heavy nipple,
Tugs like a puppy, grunting as he feeds:
Through his frail nerves her own deep languors ripple
Like a broad river sighing through its reeds.

Yet in that drowsy stream his flesh imbibes
An old unquenched unsmotherable heat—
The curbed ferocity of beaten tribes,
The sullen dignity of their defeat.

Her body looms above him like a hill
Within whose shade a village lies at rest,
Or the first cloud so terrible and still
That bears the coming harvest in its breast.

TO A PET COBRA

With breath indrawn and every nerve alert,
As at the brink of some profound abyss,
I love on my bare arm, capricious flirt,
To feel the chilly and incisive kiss
Of your lithe tongue that forks its swift caress
Between the folded slumber of your fangs,
And half reveals the nacreous recess
Where death upon those dainty hinges hangs.

Our lonely lives in every chance agreeing,
It is no common friendship that you bring,
It was the desert starved us into being,
The hate of men that sharpened us to sting:
Sired by starvation, suckled by neglect,
Hate was the surly tutor of our youth:
I too can hiss the hair of men erect
Because my lips are venomous with truth.

Where the hard rock is barren, scorched the spring,
Shrivelled the grass, and the hot wind of death
Hornets the crag with whirred metallic wing—
We drew the fatal secret of our breath:
By whirlwinds bugled forth, whose funnelled suction
Scrolls the spun sand into a golden spire,
Our spirits leaped, hosannas of destruction,
Like desert lilies forked with tongues of fire.

Dainty one, deadly one, whose folds are panthered
With stars, my slender Kalihari flower,
Whose lips with fangs are delicately anthered,
Whose coils are volted with electric power,
I love to think how men of my dull nation
Might spurn your sleep with inadvertent heel
To kindle up the lithe retaliation
And caper to the slash of sudden steel.

There is no sea so wide, no waste so sterile
But holds a rapture for the sons of strife:
There shines upon the topmost peak of peril
A throne for spirits that abound in life:
There is no joy like theirs who fight alone,
Whom lust or gluttony has never tied,
Who in their purity have built a throne,
And in their solitude a tower of pride.

I wish my life, O suave and silent sphinx,
Might flow like yours in some such strenuous line,
My days the scales, my years the bony links
That chain the length of its resilient spine:
And when at last the moment comes to strike,
Such venom give my hilted fangs the power,
Like drilling roots the dirty soil that spike,
To sting these rotted wastes into a flower.

THE ALBATROSS

(TO F. DE FREMINVILLE)

Stretching white wings in strenuous repose,
Sleeving them in the silver frills of sleep,
As I was carried, far from other foes,
To shear the long horizons of the deep,

A swift ship struck me down: through gusty glooms
I spun from fierce collision with her spars:
Shrill through the sleety pallor of my plumes
Whistled the golden bullets of the stars:

Loose on the gale my shattered wreck was strewn
And, conquered by the envious winds at last,
A rag upon the red horns of the moon,
Was tossed and gored and trampled by the blast.

Flapping the water like a sodden flag,
No more to rise, shot down by stormy guns,
How shamefully these great sprained sinews drag
That bracketed my purpose with the sun's. . . .

To the dark ocean I had dealt my laws
And when the shores rolled by, their speed was mine:
The ranges moved like long two-handled saws
Notching the scarlet west with jagged line:

Swerved like a thin blue scythe, and smoothly reaping
Their mushroom minarets and toadstool towers,

My speed had set the steel horizon sweeping
And razed the Indies like a field of flowers:

Feathered with palm and eyed with broad lagoons,
Fanned open to the dimly-burning sky,
A peacock-train of fierce mesmeric moons,
The coast of Africa had rustled by:

The broad curve of the west, with nightward tilt,
Wheeled down, and nations stood upon their crowns:
Each tower a crutch, each chimney-stack a stilt,
Across the nether sky, their fog-red towns

Went striding—while up far opposing seas
I by earth's sunward wheel was steeply borne
To see the green foam-heaved antipodes
Capsize their thousand islands on the morn.

Then through the gloom wherein, like tiny spiders
Webbed in their flimsy rays, the systems spawn,
Up dim blue rocks of cloud, with scarlet fibres,
Crawled the gigantic lichens of the dawn;

Striped with the fiery colours of the sky,
Tigered with war-paint, ramping as they rolled,
The green waves charged the sunrise letting fly
Their porpoises like boomerangs of gold.

Exploding from white cotton-pods of cloud
I saw the tufted gulls before me blow,

The black cape-hens beneath me, and the proud
White gannet in his parachute of snow.

The cliff-ringed islands where the penguins nest
Sheltered their drowsy legions from the foam
When evening brought the cormorants to rest,
Gondolas of the tempest, steering home:

To sleep or cackle, grouped in homely rings,
I left them roosting warm in their own dung,
And while they fattened there, with homeless wings
The great harp of the hurricanes I strung:

Towering far up amid the red star-sockets,
I saw deep down, in vast flotillas shoaled,
The phosphorescent whales, like bursting rockets,
Bore through the gloom their long ravines of gold.

Far coral islands rose in faint relief,
Each with its fringe of palms and shut lagoon,
Where, with a running fuse of spray, the reef
Set off the golden crackers of the moon.

By nameless capes, where the slow thunder prowls,
I dared the shapeless phantoms of the night,
Relentless as the noon to dazzled owls,
Inflicting beauty on their hate of light.

Squelching like sodden shoes, with canvas trailing,
Doomed vessels swung their teetering yards on high,

Or downward as they plunged, with syrens wailing,
Reared to the stars their tempest-throttled cry.

I read my doom in those great shattered ribs
Nor with vague fancies drugged my truth-of-sight,
I knew the stars for momentary squibs
In the perpetual horror of the night:

I saw how vile a thing it is to die
Save when careering on their sunward course,
The strong heart cracks, the shivered senses fly,
Stunned by their own expenditure of force.

Erect, unterrified, though robbed of breath,
In those wild hours of triumph had I died,
The shades around, as in a meteor's death,
Had seen annihilation glorified.

My stiff quills made the hurricane their lyre
Where, pronged with azure flame, the black rain
        streams:
Huge brindled shadows barred with gloomy fire
Prowling the red horizon of my dreams,

Thick storm-clouds threatened me with dense eclipse,
The wind made whirling rowels of the stars—
Over black waves where sky-careering ships
Gibbet the moon upon their crazy spars,

42

From bow-bent wings I shot my white resilience
Grazing the tempest like a shaft of light,
Till with the sunrise, shivering into trillions
Of winged fish, I saw the wave ignite.

Through calms that seemed the swoon of all the
    gales,
On snowy frills that softest winds had spun,
I floated like a seed with silken sails
Out of the sleepy thistle of the sun.

I had been dashed in the gold spray of dawns,
And hit with silver by the stars' faint light,
The red moon charged at me with lowered horns,
Buffalo-shouldered by the gloom of night:

Broidering earth's senseless matter with my sight,
Weaving my life around it like a robe,
Onward I draw my silken clues of flight,
Spooled by the wheeling glories of the globe.

The world, revolving like a vast cocoon,
Unwound its threading leagues at my desire:
With burning stitches by the sun and moon
My life was woven like a shawl of fire—

Clashing the surf-white fringe that round it runs,
Its giant mesh of fire-shot silk, unfurled
And braided with a chain of flashing suns,
Fleeces the craggy shoulders of the world:

43

How dimly now its threads are ravelled out,
Its gorgeous colours smoulder from my brain,
While my numbed memory, the world about,
Rays forth its thin meridians of pain.

My eyes with wild funereal trophies blaze
Like dying torches—spoils of azure nights
And the slain suns my speed has shorn of rays
And dashed to bleed upon the western heights.

Night surges up the black reef of the world,
Shaking the skies in ponderous collapse,
I hear the long horizons, steeply hurled,
Rush cataracting down through starless gaps.

No more to rise, the last sun bombs the deep
And strews my shattered senses with its light—
My spirit knows the silence it must keep
And with the ocean hankers for the night.

IN THE TOWN SQUARE

To those who lingered out of doors
The Night was cold: in trance of lead
The Town slept save for thieves and whores,
A poet, and the watchful dead.

Even the moon withheld her gold,
The teller, Night, through cloudy bars,
Into his sack with fingers cold
Counted his scanty change of stars.

Numbed scarecrows slept on either hand,
Once human, whom through changing moons
The nameless hungers of the land
Had hunted into gaunt baboons.

Out of the ghastly Cenotaph
That next the Lavatory looms,
The echo of a ghostly laugh
Came rolling from the world of tombs,

And in its wake faint whispers whirred
Like startled bats some gust might stir
In a long tunnel: there I heard
The ghostly myrmidons confer;

The friends that once, superbly mounted,
Had laughed and galloped by my side

Now some sad mystery recounted
To which the hollow vault replied.

Voice after voice, as when by night
The crickets call, or from a mine
Long water-logged, with plaintive flight,
The shrill mosquitoes upward whine—

Faint, insect-like and thin it came,
The wistful sound those heroes made,
Ferreted down by Deathless Fame
Into the warrens of the shade.

Between the marble and the metal
I heard their reedy voices pipe,
Where the blue-burnished angels settle
Like flies upon a slab of tripe.

Then one by one they ceased to quire,
As when a storm-cloud shades the West
The shaven poets of the mire
Their marshy music hush to rest.

The Town slept on. So cheaply fine
Its walls embalmed its festered soul—
But far along the sky's red line
There seemed a quiet mist to roll,

The soul of Africa, the grey
Hushed emanation of her hills,

The drowsy poison of her day,
The hand that fondles while it kills,

The subtle anæsthetic breath,
The vengeful sting that gives no pain
But deals around it worse than death
The palsied soul, the mildewed brain.

TO A YOUNG MAN WITH PINK EYES

Indigenous to realms unreal
Where such necessities are free
As only through our wounds we feel
And only through our tears may see,
Through the fair garden of your mind
Whistles the blue flight of the dove,
A sound of bees pervades the wind
And vegetables making love.

Narcissus of what lilied pool,
In what fair Eden do you sigh?
Out of its mirror clear and cool
What bullfrog ogles you to die?
What guarantee do you embody,
O ace of automatic hearts,
O patent soul, asbestos body,
And brain of unassembled parts?

The feathered cupidons divert you
And shady groves delight your eyes
Far from the icy crags of virtue,
Where only eagles dare to rise:
In equanimity you plunge
The rosy flannel of your sight,
And with boracic vision sponge
The irritation of the light.

While the soft fondant of your eye
Adhesive to all comfort stays,
Mine like a lighthouse round the sky
Swivels its fierce tormented rays,
And while those flagging fins, your ears,
Flounder you gently down the scale,
My own among the whirling spheres
Propel me like an angry whale.

Into my Paradise whose bound,
A ridge of rocks without a tree,
By fiery clouds is circled round
And washed with thunder by the sea,
Experience, warding the grey gates,
A gorgon with erected crest,
Admits the cold infernal hates
Whose company I love the best.

Unguarded by the sword of Michael,
The fruit of knowledge tempts the tooth,
And on their tyres of moonlight cycle
The hissing cobras of the truth:
There Power, among the gloomy hills,
Electric in the panther burns,
And Wisdom in the python rills
A stream of starlight through the ferns.

Each to himself a holy book
How vainly we mythologize,

When but a difference in the look
Adjusts the difference in the eyes—
For though as steel to pork impinge
Our looks, O youth of little guile,
Why is it I with pain who twinge,
And you unfeelingly who smile?

AFRICAN MOONRISE

The wind with fœtid muzzle sniffed its feast,
The carrion town, that lulled its crowds to rest
Like the sprawled carcase of some giant beast
That hives the rustling larvæ in its breast.

When the cold moon rose glinting from the fen
And snailed her slime of fire along the hill,
Insomnia, the Muse of angry men,
To other themes had chid my faithless quill.

But wide I flung the shutters on their hinges
And watched the moon as from the gilded mire
Where the black river trails its reedy fringes,
She fished her shadow with a line of fire.

Against her light the dusty palms were charred:
The frogs, her faithless troubadours, were still,
Alone, it seemed, I kept my trusty guard
Over the stone-grey silence of the hill,

Till a starved mongrel tugging at his chain
With fearful jerks, hairless and wide of eye,
From where he crouched, a thrilling spear of pain,
Hurled forth his Alleluia to the sky.

Fierce tremors volted through his bony notches
And shook the skirling bag-pipe of his hide—

Beauty has still one faithful heart who watches,
One last Endymion left to hymn her pride!

Sing on, lone voice! make all the desert ring,
My listening spirit kindles and adores . . .
Such were my voice, had I the heart to sing,
But mine should be a fiercer howl than yours!

SILENCE

I know your footfall hushed and frail,
Fair siren of the snow-born lake
Whose surface only swans should sail
And only silver hymns should break,
Or thankful prayers devout as this
White trophy of a night of sighs
Where Psyche celebrates the kiss
With which a sister closed her eyes.

THE FESTIVALS OF FLIGHT

Too sensitively nerved to bear
Domestication, O my friends
On a perpetual change of air
Whose sole stability depends,

By what phenomenal emotion,
Alas, is each of us obsessed
That travel, flight, and ceaseless motion
Must keep us in a state of rest?

Schooled by the new gymnastic Muse
In barbarous academies,
The rifle and the running noose
Conferred upon us their degrees,

To play our more precarious parts
Trapezed above the rolling decks
Or in the high equestrian arts
To graduate with broken necks.

Yet I could wish, before I perish,
To make my peace with God above
Or, like a millionaire, to cherish
My purse with soft marsupial love,

Or like a poet woo the moon,
Riding an arm-chair for my steed,

And with a flashing pen harpoon
Terrific metaphors of speed—

Speed, motion, flight!—the last hosanna
Of routed angels: sword that fights
The coward free: unfailing manna
Of earth's fastidious Israelites!

Valise of invalids on tour:
Refuge of refugees in flight:
Home of the homeless: sinecure
Of hunted thieves at dead of night.

Nirvana of the record-breakers,
Heaven in which our senses swim,
Aviary of aviators
And poultry-run of seraphim!

Safari to the unexplored
With rough first-aid for Cupid's darts,
Perambulator of the Bored
And ambulance of broken hearts!

Deranger of the intellects
Of those who flee before a curse,
Fixative of blurred effects,
And laxative of minor verse!

Mecca of all mechanic progress:
Destination, course, and goal

Of those who've none: Circean Ogress
Whose snouted trophy is my soul!

Tourist, who leaves with ten-league boots
His spoor of Castles down the Rhine:
Smoker of immense cheroots—
The funnels of the Cunard Line!

Of cranks, the boomerang and waddy:
Of rogues, the assegai and kerry:
Black Maria to the Body,
To the Soul a Stygian ferry!

Pope of the gypsies: sole religion
Of those who sail with every breeze:
The Son, the Father, and the Pigeon
Of wandering aborigines!

To Thee our heathen hymns are hurled
From where we wander in the clouds—
Sonatas on the fog-horn skirled,
The pibroch of the creaking shrouds.

Lead, kindly ignis fatuus, far
Amid the world's encircling gloom:
In my last trek be thou the star
To whom I hitch my disselboom.

Far from the famed memorial arch
Towards a lonely grave I come,

My heart in its funereal march
Goes beating like a muffled drum,

Yet lest when midnight winds are loud
I should not see the way to go,
Let every gross proverbial cloud
Its shabby silver lining show:

And you shall lend me, if you please,
That in the mode I may appear,
Your shirt, tormented Hercules!
Laocoön! your bandolier.

POETS IN AFRICA

(TO W. PLOMER)

For grazing innocence a salad
Of lilies in the bud,
For those who dine on words a ballad,
For you and me a name of mud,
A rash of stars upon the sky,
A pox of flowers on the earth—
To such diseases of the eye
Habituated from our birth,

We had no time for make-believe
So early each began
To wear his liver on his sleeve,
To snarl, and be an angry man:
Far in the desert we have been
Where Nature, still to poets kind,
Admits no vegetable green
To soften the determined mind,

But with snarled gold and rumbled blue
Must disinfect the sight
Where once the tender maggots grew
Of faith and beauty and delight.
Each with a blister on his tongue,
Each with a crater in his tooth,
Our nerves are fire: we have been stung
By the tarantulas of truth.

Each like a freezing salamander
Impervious and immune,
No snivelling sentiment shall pander
To our flirtations with the moon,
And though with gay batrachian chirrup
Her poets thrill the swampy reach,
Not with so glutinous a syrup
As moonlight shall we grease our speech.

Our cook, the Sun, in craggy kitchens
Amid the howling waste
Has fried the terrible sour lichens
So dainty to a poet's taste,
Which sovereign remedy is ours
Against the earth's infectious scars,
Its annual eczema of flowers
The pullulation of its stars—

Whose itch corrodes the soft medulla
Of kindlier brains than ours
Wherein, attuned to local colour,
Each cheap colonial virtue flowers,
Flits like a moth from bloom to blossom
Or to protective markings trusts,
In shady corners playing possum
To gratify its private lusts.

The fauna of this mental waste,
They cheer our lonely way

And round our doleful footsteps haste
To skip, to gambol, and to play;
The kite of Mercy sails above
With reeking claws and cry that clangs,
The old grey wolf of Brother-Love
Slinks in our track with yellow fangs.

And it is sweet at times to hear,
Out of the turf we trod,
Hysterical with pain and fear,
The blood of Abel screech to God,
Hurled shivering up through vaults immense
Where, whirling round the empty sky,
Green fossils of Omnipotence,
The bones of his Creator fly.

True sons of Africa are we,
Though bastardized with culture,
Indigenous, and wild, and free
As wolf, as pioneer and vulture—
Yea, though for us the vision blearing
No membrane nictitates the light,
Though we are cursed with sense and hearing
And doubly cursed with second sight,

Still doomed that skyward screech to hear
That haunted us in youth,
We shall grow terrible through fear,
We shall grow venomous with truth,

And through these plains where thought meanders
Through sheepish brains in wormy life,
Our lives shall roll like fierce Scamanders
Their red alluvium of strife.

When in the moonlight, red and bloody,
The night has smeared the plain,
We rise from awful nights of study
With coal-red eyes and whirling brain—
Our minds like dark destructive engines
Prepare those catapults and slings
In whose preliminary vengeance
The thunder of the Future sings.

What though we have no walls or bastions
To shield our riddled hearts?—
Arrowed like convicts, twin Sebastians
Each in his uniform of darts,
When in his crimson garb outlandish
The martyr turns a porcupine
Who such fearful spikes can brandish,
Who in more fiendish war-paint shine?

THE ZEBRAS

From the dark woods that breathe of fallen showers,
Harnessed with level rays in golden reins,
The zebras draw the dawn across the plains
Wading knee-deep among the scarlet flowers.
The sunlight, zithering their flanks with fire,
Flashes between the shadows as they pass
Barred with electric tremors through the grass
Like wind along the gold strings of a lyre.

Into the flushed air snorting rosy plumes
That smoulder round their feet in drifting fumes,
With dove-like voices call the distant fillies,
While round the herds the stallion wheels his flight,
Engine of beauty volted with delight,
To roll his mare among the trampled lilies.

TRISTAN DA CUNHA

Snore in the foam; the night is vast and blind;
The blanket of the mist about your shoulders,
Sleep your old sleep of rock, snore in the wind,
Snore in the spray! the storm your slumber lulls,
His wings are folded on your nest of boulders
As on their eggs the grey wings of your gulls.

No more as when, so dark an age ago,
You hissed a giant cinder from the ocean,
Around your rocks you furl the shawling snow
Half sunk in your own darkness, vast and grim,
And round you on the deep with surly motion
Pivot your league-long shadow as you swim.

Why should you haunt me thus but that I know
My surly heart is in your own displayed,
Round whom such leagues in endless circuit flow,
Whose hours in such a gloomy compass run—
A dial with its league-long arm of shade
Slowly revolving to the moon and sun.

My pride has sunk, like your grey fissured crags,
By its own strength o'ertoppled and betrayed:
I, too, have burned the wind with fiery flags
Who now am but a roost for empty words,
An island of the sea whose only trade
Is in the voyages of its wandering birds.

Did you not, when your strength became your pyre,
Deposed and tumbled from your flaming tower,
Awake in gloom from whence you sank in fire,
To find, Antæus-like, more vastly grown,
A throne in your own darkness, and a power
Sheathed in the very coldness of your stone?

Your strength is that you have no hope or fear,
You march before the world without a crown,
The nations call you back, you do not hear,
The cities of the earth grow grey behind you,
You will be there when their great flames go down
And still the morning in the van will find you.

You march before the continents, you scout
In front of all the earth; alone you scale
The mast-head of the world, a lorn look-out,
Waving the snowy flutter of your spray
And gazing back in infinite farewell
To suns that sink and shores that fade away.

From your grey tower what long regrets you fling
To where, along the low horizon burning,
The great swan-breasted seraphs soar and sing,
And suns go down, and trailing splendours dwindle,
And sails on lonely errands unreturning
Glow with a gold no sunrise can rekindle.

Turn to the night; these flames are not for you
Whose steeple for the thunder swings its bells;
Grey Memnon, to the tempest only true,
Turn to the night, turn to the shadowing foam,
And let your voice, the saddest of farewells,
With sullen curfew toll the grey wings home.

The wind, your mournful syren, haunts the gloom;
The rocks, spray-clouded, are your signal guns
Whose stony nitre, puffed with flying spume,
Rolls forth in grim salute your broadside hollow
Over the gorgeous burials of suns
To sound the tocsin of the storms that follow.

Plunge forward like a ship to battle hurled,
Slip the long cables of the failing light,
The level rays that moor you to the world:
Sheathed in your armour of eternal frost,
Plunge forward, in the thunder of the fight
To lose yourself as I would fain be lost.

Exiled like you and severed from my race
By the cold ocean of my own disdain,
Do I not freeze in such a wintry space,
Do I not travel through a storm as vast
And rise at times, victorious from the main,
To fly the sunrise at my shattered mast?

Your path is but a desert where you reap
Only the bitter knowledge of your soul:
You fish with nets of seaweed in the deep
As fruitlessly as I with nets of rhyme—
Yet forth you stride, yourself the way, the goal,
The surges are your strides, your path is time.

Hurled by what aim to what tremendous range!
A missile from the great sling of the past,
Your passage leaves its track of death and change
And ruin on the world: you fly beyond
Leaping the current of the ages vast
As lightly as a pebble skims a pond.

The years are undulations in your flight
Whose awful motion we can only guess—
Too swift for sense, too terrible for sight,
We only know how fast behind you darken
Our days like lonely beacons of distress:
We know that you stride on and will not harken.

Now in the eastern sky the fairest planet
Pierces the dying wave with dangled spear,
And in the whirring hollows of your granite
That vaster sea to which you are a shell
Sighs with a ghostly rumour, like the drear
Moan of the nightwind in a hollow cell.

We shall not meet again; over the wave
Our ways divide, and yours is straight and endless,
But mine is short and crooked to the grave:
Yet what of these dark crowds amid whose flow
I battle like a rock, aloof and friendless,
Are not their generations vague and endless
The waves, the strides, the feet on which I go?

THE SISTERS

After hot loveless nights, when cold winds stream
Sprinkling the frost and dew, before the light,
Bored with the foolish things that girls must dream
Because their beds are empty of delight,

Two sisters rise and strip. Out from the night
Their horses run to their low-whistled pleas—
Vast phantom shapes with eyeballs rolling white
That sneeze a fiery stream about their knees:

Through the crisp manes their stealthy prowling
    hands,
Stronger than curbs, in slow caresses rove,
They gallop down across the milk-white sands
And wade far out into the sleeping cove:

The frost stings sweetly with a burning kiss
As intimate as love, as cold as death:
Their lips, whereon delicious tremors hiss,
Fume with the ghostly pollen of their breath.

Far out on the grey silence of the flood
They watch the dawn in smouldering gyres expand
Beyond them: and the day burns through their blood
Like a white candle through a shuttered hand.

RESURRECTION

The sun leaves rosy with his breath
A heaven rinsed with silver rains,
And on the golden verge of death
The lingering storm in glory gains:

While the red light and rolling thunder
Unvanquished from their fight withdraw:
Dim to the eyes' yet vibrant wonder
Whom such a vision held in awe,

Exhaling in the mists of gold
From every pollen-wreathèd husk,
His triumphs in the stars foretold,
A shade emerges in the dusk,

A wrestler such as Jacob knew
Whose strength increases with the hours,
A Hercules of matchless thew
Whose body is the breath of flowers—

So evening with a god grew full
When Jove, amid such blossomed thorns,
Raised, in the lily-breathing Bull,
The silver moonrise of his horns.

Antæus of the fallen storms,
The resurrection of the power
Whose splendours in the frailest forms
The most unconquerably tower,

The Form whose challenge, high and loud,
The whistling fifes of wind had spun,
Whose rolling muscles to a proud
Repulse had dared the noonday sun,

Whose heavy torrent-hurling shock
Had filled the roaring gullies, bowed
The groaning tree, and split the rock—
Had worn no armour but a cloud,

And now from the wet earth reborn,
All Africa his phoenix pyre,
Out of a thousand leagues of thorn
Had softly smouldered into fire.

The lightning sinews of his limbs
Are in that soft effulgence furled
And on the breath of incense swims
The thunderbolt his anger hurled.

Diffusing on through endless space,
Majestic peace without a flaw,
Wild is the light that from his face
The woods and dreaming waters draw.

The skies are with his trophies hung—
The Bull, the Lion, and the Bear;
What spoil of victories unsung
Remains to be erected there?

The gorgeous Ram that horns his lyre
Of silence: whose great pelt is rolled
To quilt a thousand hills with fire
In the acacia's fleece of gold—

Round which, astream through flowering vales,
Dread guardians, pythoning the spoils,
Lit by the moon with glittering scales
The great Zambezis wreathe their coils—

Shorn from the shoulders of the morning
By his strong arm of thunder, yields
Its shaggy hide, his thews adorning
In all the fragrance of the fields.

Yet through the wreaths of cloudy fire
That crown the hazard of his quest,
Still to new victories aspire
The broodings of his dark unrest.

And his long gaze, down some immense
Horizon of horizons drawn,
Yearns to the fleeced magnificence
And fire of its perennial dawn.

Short is the peace, though hushed and breathless,
In which we feel the victor's will
And its intrinsic hydra, deathless,
Reviving at the self-same rill.

TO A CONTEMPORARY

Around the galleries you frame,
Forbid to smoke or spit,
Dark repetitions of the same
Derisive demon sit—
Far in the pit his faces glimmer,
Shirt-fronted in the stalls,
His myriad spectacles a-shimmer
Confront the lighted halls:
One Hydra throngs the loaded stands,
One Argus gives the glance,
One Briareus claps the hands
When down the stage the dance,
Trumpeted on by fiery lights
With fanfares of phlogiston,
Tarantulates in scarlet tights
For flashing arms to piston.
Their breasts ballooned with lust and song,
The fat sopranos kick—
Nor does one false manœuvre wrong
That strict arithmetic;
Upon a simultaneous heel
Your sorrows learned their drill,
To kick as high, as swiftly wheel,
And sing as falsely shrill.

THE SLEEPER

She lies so still, her only motion
The waves of hair that round her sweep
Revolving to their hushed explosion
Of fragrance on the shores of sleep.
Is it my spirit or her flesh
That takes this breathless, silver swoon?
Sleep has no darkness to enmesh
That lonely rival of the moon,
Her beauty, vigilant and white,
That wakeful through the long blue night,
Watches, with my own sleepless eyes,
The darkness silver into day,
And through their sockets burns away
The sorrows that have made them wise.

AMPHISBOENA

1ST HEAD

Give place to me, presumptuous sequel,
I from the egg was first to come.

2ND HEAD

Till time can prove our forces equal
Your face must dangle at my bum.

1ST HEAD

At every notch upon my spine
Has hung a better head than you,
I string such beads upon a line
And thread with skulls my endless clue.
Snap but the single slender sinew
Which centuries to link us spun,
And you must cease, while I continue
Coeval with the moon and sun.
I am the ever-full clepsydra
From which such drops as you must flow,
My eyes are Argus, heads are hydra,
Though masked a single face to show.
Still as it lengthens growing slenderer
Though motion to your end may go,
Scolopendra, scolopendra,
The regimental minutes flow
To mine, restoring all you steal:

For every inch you gain in space,
I wind a year upon my reel
And am the winner of the race.

2ND HEAD

Yet while I can I'll move in front,
As long as I've the strength to haul.
Your only science is to shunt,
That is, if you can move at all!
You cannot scare me with such notions,
Or fright me with a mask of stone—
Your glaring, that would freeze my motions,
Is yet Medusa to your own.

HORSES ON THE CAMARGUE

In the grey wastes of dread,
The haunt of shattered gulls where nothing moves
But in a shroud of silence like the dead,
I heard a sudden harmony of hooves,
And, turning, saw afar
A hundred snowy horses unconfined,
The silver runaways of Neptune's car
Racing, spray-curled, like waves before the wind.
Sons of the Mistral, fleet
As him with whose strong gusts they love to flee,
Who shod the flying thunders on their feet
And plumed them with the snortings of the sea;
Theirs is no earthly breed
Who only haunt the verges of the earth
And only on the sea's salt herbage feed—
Surely the great white breakers gave them birth.
For when for years a slave,
A horse of the Camargue, in alien lands,
Should catch some far-off fragrance of the wave
Carried far inland from his native sands,
Many have told the tale
Of how in fury, foaming at the rein,
He hurls his rider; and with lifted tail,
With coal-red eyes and cataracting mane,
Heading his course for home,
Though sixty foreign leagues before him sweep,
Will never rest until he breathes the foam

And hears the native thunder of the deep.
But when the great gusts rise
And lash their anger on these arid coasts,
When the scared gulls career with mournful cries
And whirl across the waste like driven ghosts:
When hail and fire converge,
The only souls to which they strike no pain
Are the white-crested fillies of the surge
And the white horses of the windy plain.
Then in their strength and pride
The stallions of the wilderness rejoice;
They feel their Master's trident in their side,
And high and shrill they answer to his voice.
With white tails smoking free,
Long streaming manes, and arching necks, they show
Their kinship to their sisters of the sea—
And forward hurl their thunderbolts of snow.
Still out of hardship bred,
Spirits of power and beauty and delight
Have ever on such frugal pastures fed
And loved to course with tempests through the night.

MASS AT DAWN

I dropped my sail and dried my dripping seines
Where the white quay is chequered by cool planes
In whose great branches, always out of sight,
The nightingales are singing day and night.
Though all was grey beneath the moon's grey beam,
My boat in her new paint shone like a bride,
And silver in my baskets shone the bream:
My arms were tired and I was heavy-eyed,
But when with food and drink, at morning-light,
The children met me at the water-side,
Never was wine so red or bread so white.

THE PALM

Blistered and dry was the desert I trod
When out of the sky with the step of a god,
Victory-vanned, with her feathers out-fanned,
The palm tree alighting my journey delayed
And spread me, inviting, her carpet of shade.
Vain were evasions, though urgent my quest,
And there as the guest of her lovely persuasions
To lie in the shade of her branches was best.
Like a fountain she played, spilling plume over
    plume in
A golden cascade for the winds to illumine,
Ascending in brilliance and falling in shade,
And spurning the ground with a tiptoe resilience,
Danced to the sound of the music she made.
Her voice intervened on my shadowed seclusion
Like the whispered intrusion of seraph or fiend,
In its tone was the hiss of the serpent's wise tongue
But soft as the kiss of a lover it stung—
"Unstrung is your lute? For despair are you silent?
Am I not an island in oceans as mute?
Around me the thorns of the desert take root;
Though I spring from the rock of a region accurst,
Yet fair is the daughter of hunger and thirst
Who sings like the water the valleys have nursed,
And rings her blue shadow as deep and as cool
As the heavens of azure that sleep on a pool.
And you, who so soon by the toil were undone,

Could you guess through what horrors my beauty
    had won
Ere I crested the moon as the bride of the sun?
The roots are my anchor struck fast in the hill,
The higher I hanker, the deeper they drill,
Through the red mortar their claws interlock
To ferret the water through warrens of rock.
Each inch of my glory was wrenched with a groan,
Corroded with fire from the base of my throne
And drawn like a wire from the heart of a stone:
Though I soar in the height with a shape of delight
Uplifting my stem like the string of a kite,
Yet still must each grade of my climbing be told
And still from the summit my measure I hold,
Sounding the azure with plummet of gold.
Partaking the strain of the heavenward pride
That soars me away from the earth I deride,
Though my stem be a rein that would tether me down
And fasten a chain on the height of my crown,
Yet through its tense nerve do I measure my might,
The strain of its curb is the strength of my flight:
And when, by the hate of the hurricane blown,
It doubles its forces with fibres that groan,
Exulting I ride in the tower of my pride
To feel that the strength of the blast is my own . . .
Rest under my branches, breathe deep of my balm
From the hushed avalanches of fragrance and calm,
For suave is the silence that poises the palm.
The wings of the egrets are silken and fine,

But hushed with the secrets of Eden are mine:
Your spirit that grieves like the wind in my leaves
Shall be robbed of its care by those whispering thieves
To study my patience and hear, the day long,
The soft foliations of sand into song—
For bitter and cold though it rasp to my root,
Each atom of gold is the chance of a fruit,
The sap is the music, the stem is the flute,
And the leaves are the wings of the seraph I shape
Who dances, who springs in a golden escape,
Out of the dust and the drought of the plain,
To sing with the silver hosannas of rain."

ESTOCADE

A clumsy bull, obscene and fat,
Who wears the devil's pointed hat
And cloven shoe,
Seems from my brain a sylph to call
To tease him with my flaming shawl
And thrust his shoulders through.

Dull eyes, like owls', that shrink away
Insulted from the light of day
In bloodshot gloom,
In my red silk see only night
And in my flame of steel no light
To glorify their doom—

No more can this blind passion claim,
Across whose blurred instinctive aim
My cloak I swung
Into a tumbled heap diverting
Its steel-shot bulk with redly-squirting
Nose and lolling tongue.

For though to frenzy still be stirred
The unwieldy lecher of the herd,
Still to its brain
I am all wings and airy lightness
And make a comet of my whiteness
In that black sky of pain.

AUTUMN

I love to see, when leaves depart,
The clear anatomy arrive,
Winter, the paragon of art,
That kills all forms of life and feeling
Save what is pure and will survive.

Already now the clanging chains
Of geese are harnessed to the moon:
Stripped are the great sun-clouding planes:
And the dark pines, their own revealing,
Let in the needles of the noon.

Strained by the gale the olives whiten
Like hoary wrestlers bent with toil
And, with the vines, their branches lighten
To brim our vats where summer lingers
In the red froth and sun-gold oil.

Soon on our hearth's reviving pyre
Their rotted stems will crumble up:
And like a ruby, panting fire,
The grape will redden on your fingers
Through the lit crystal of the cup.

AN OPEN WINDOW

An open window where the blue
Wind washed the snowy flowers with dew,
My lateness to deride,
Across my sunken pillow threw
The morning's silver pride
When I from sullen dreams awoke
And to my doubts, before they spoke,
Unbidden thoughts replied—

"We were not idle though you slept
But, secret spiders, we have kept
The track of wasted hours:
In corners you had left unswept
The busy toil was ours
By which, before the dawn was red,
A thousand suns of silk were spread
To catch the falling showers.

"Our webs are lit with stars of dew:
Pulleyed with pearls, each frosty clue
Its maze of glory runs,
While we, reflecting every hue,
As eager as the Sons
Of Morning to exalt their Sire,
Shoot forth our rays of liquid fire
To multiply the sun's.

"Before the lark had left the corn,
Your love had bathed, and to the morn
Was up to show the way:
We saw how with her blood the dawn
Had fused its silver ray
Till on your bed's cool-quilted snows,
Flushed as the phantom of a rose,
Her lighted shadow lay.

"Nor slow to follow in her way
See how, in lovely disarray,
New hope, with limbs aglow,
Stands at the chilly brink of day
And hesitating so,
In that clear current, half in fright
At the swift tremor of delight,
Has dipped a rosy toe."

SONNET

The teeth of pleasure, when they hiss
So fiercely through the rasping rind,
Reach but the verges of that bliss
The fruit has lost its form to find.
The fruit's a fiction of the mind
Whose scent and taste our senses miss,
Save when, to fiery thought refined,
They draw a fragrance from your kiss
As thrilling as the deep-drawn breath
With which the blood begins to flare
When life is triggered by a hair
And stands upon the peak of death,
Elate, with scarlet cloak outspread,
Before a bull with lowered head.

THE GARDEN

Where not a breeze the silence raids
And by the outer noon forgot,
Strayed sunbeams crack with ruby shot
The smooth gold rind of the grenades:
Lit only by the falling stream,
The Form familiar to my rest
With fluid arm and naked breast
Flushes the crystal of my theme,
Yet on its clearness sheds no haze
Of sorrow more than if a glass
Between me and the sun should pass
To share the unimpeded rays.
Soft fall the laurel-scented hours
Rinsed with the golden light, and long
For those in faith and virtue strong
Shall rain upon their bed of flowers:
While through its falls of silver sheer
Ascends the music of the spring
With fluted throat and jewelled wing
To sing as ever through the year,
How Love was like a Laurel sprung
Within whose quiet ring of shade
Beauty and Wit, like man and maid,
Have lain as we since earth was young—
While all the crowns that glory weaves
To buckle on victorious brows
Were offered for their tent of boughs,

Around whose stillness vainly grieves
The valour that has daunted time,
And all the deathless flow of rhyme
Is but a wind among the leaves.

THE SNAKE

(TO LIAM O'FLAHERTY)

Damp clods with corn may thank the showers,
But when the desert boulder flowers
No common buds unfold—
A Jove to Danaë's bridal showers
Immortal fire and gold,
And high above the wastes will tower
The hydra stem, the deathless flower.

A glory, such as from scant seed
The thirsty rocks suffice to breed
Out of the rainless glare,
Was born in me of such a need
And of a like despair,
But fairer than the aloe sprang
And hilted with a sharper fang.

The heart whom shame or anger sears
Beyond the cheap relief of tears
Its secret never opes,
Save to the loveliest of fears,
The most divine of hopes,
And only when such seeds may find
A tough resistance in the rind—

Hard husks the self-same truth express
As, yielding to the sweet excess

Of hoarded gems within,
They crack to show the rich recess
Our thirsty lips would win,
When ripe grenades that drink the sun
Resolving into rubies run.

So from the old Anchises' tomb
All that the fire could not consume,
The living ichor, flowed,
A serpent from the rocky womb
Where barren death abode,
With lifted crest and radiant gyre
Revolving into wheels of fire.

No rock so pure a crystal rears
But filed with water, thawed with years,
Or by its prophet struck,
Its breast may sparkle into tears
For thirsting hordes to suck.
But it was to a sorer dint
And flashing from a harder flint

That, smitten by its angry god,
My heart recoiling to the rod
Rilled forth its stream of pride,
A serpent from the rifted clod
On rolling wheels to ride,
Who reared, as if their birth were one,
To gaze, an equal, on the Sun.

His eyes like slots of jet inlaid
On their smooth triangle of jade,
Were vigilant with fire,
His armour stripped the sun for braid
And wore the stars for tire
And slid the glory of its greaves
A stream of moonlight through the leaves.

Immortal longings hold his sight
Still sunward to that source of light
Drained from whose crystal spars
His slender current rolls its bright
Alluvium of stars,
And through its winding channel trails
The shingle of his burnished scales.

The news that such a king was crowned
Has made a solitude around
His vigil hushed and calm,
Where, with the fruits of Eden wound,
He girds the stripling Palm
And shares her starry shade with none
Save with the silence and the sun.

His teeth stained crimson with her flowers,
There through the blue enchanted hours
Rocked by the winds to rest,
Her fragrance lulls his folded powers
When slumber sinks his crest

Through his own circles clear and cool
As through the ripples of a pool.

A crystal freshet through whose sluice
The noonday beams their light reduce
To one melodious line,
And flow together like the juice
That circles in the vine,
His frosty ichor drinks the sun
And fuses fire and ice in one.

When by the horror-breathing wraith
The soul is scorched of hope and faith,
This form survives the fire,
The living self no flame can scathe,
The spine, the ringing wire
That silver through its alloy sings
And fresh in each exertion springs.

Blest is the stony ground, where smite
No rains but of the angry light,
And rich beyond all dreams,
Whose stubborn seed will not ignite
Save to such deathless beams
As first through emeralds fire did ray
And into diamonds shot the day:

And blest exchange for vain delight,
For dreams, the tyrants of the night,

And passions—of the day,
Is his whose clear, unchanging sight
Through triumph, change, decay,
In such a serpent's coiled repose
His secret architecture knows.

SATIRICAL FRAGMENTS

HOME THOUGHTS IN
BLOOMSBURY

Of all the clever people round me here
I most delight in Me—
Mine is the only voice I care to hear,
And mine the only face I like to see.

THE TRUTH ABOUT RHODES

His friends contend that Rhodes is with the saints,
His foes consign him to the Stygian shore;
But all who see him here in Roworth's paints
Will gasp for brandy and dispute no more.

HOLISM

The love of Nature burning in his heart,
Our new Saint Francis offers us his book—
The saint who fed the birds at Bondleswaart
And fattened up the vultures at Bull Hoek.

A TEMPERANCE OFFICIAL AT THE EXHIBITION OF SOUTH AFRICAN PAINTINGS

He stares entranced on sunsets, clouds, and plains,
With rapture eyes the mountains and the rivers—
He's taking tips for diagrams of brains
And charts of swollen livers.

BLACK MAGIC

("H. Wodson, a name to conjure with in the journalistic
world"—*Natal Advertiser*, edited by H. Wodson.)

Sound the dread word. Beelzebub, appear!
For Wodson's name is written on the wall.
The door gapes open, hush, what have we here?
. . . Only a printer's devil after all.

ON SOME SOUTH AFRICAN NOVELISTS

You praise the firm restraint with which they write—
I'm with you there, of course:
They use the snaffle and the curb all right,
But where's the bloody horse?

ON THE SAME

Far from the vulgar haunts of men
Each sits in her "successful room",
Housekeeping with her fountain pen
And writing novels with her broom.

POLYBIUS JUBB, AS VEGETARIAN

A globular highbrow I knew
Who had an aversion for stew,
But sad to relate
The less that he ate
The Laager and Laager he grew.

POLYBIUS JUBB'S DEFENCE OF
HIGHBROWS

There once came a highbrow from Britain
Whose praises can never be written,
So steep rose his highbrow
From his heel to his eyebrow,
With a bump in the middle to sit on.

99

THE LAND-GRABBER

ON A POET WHO OFFERED HIS HEART FOR
A HANDFUL OF SOUTH AFRICAN SOIL

The bargain is fair and the bard is no robber,
A handful of dirt for a heartful of slobber.

ON THE DEATH OF A JOURNALIST

Angels received his dying breath,
This last kind act his spirit shrives;
He has done more good by his death
Than could a saint with fifty lives.

ON PROFESSOR DRENNAN'S VERSE

Who forced the Muse to this alliance?
A Man of more degrees than parts—
The jilted Bachelor of Science
And Widower of Arts.

THE DEATH OF POLYBIUS JUBB

He died in attempting to swallow,
Which proves that, though fat, he was hollow—
For in gasping for space
He swallowed his face,
And hadn't the courage to follow.

NOTES

ADAMASTOR

The spirit of the Cape whose apparition and prophecy form one of the finest passages in "The Lusiad" of Camoëns.

A VELD ECLOGUE

Jiggers. Subcutaneous parasites.

Ferreira. A smutty folk-song in Afrikaans.

Nagmaal. A reunion of South African peasants and their families for purposes of social festivity, commerce and religious debauchery.

Empire Group. A society whose meetings are mentally and morally analogous to the above.

Bolitho. Hector, not William. Prolific and popular interpreter of the "New Earth," the "Open Spaces," etc., to which he even relates the present writer's poems. Accounting for the mental and physical "superiority" of the Colonial to the European, B. writes—" 'It's the distance that does it,' said my millionaire, looking at me with his rather fine head chiselled on a background of cream madonna-lilies, 'it's the distance that does it.' "

"Totius." *Nom de plume* of a popular Afrikaans bard. His masterpiece, *Die Os* (the Ox), is highly praised by Dr. Hermann, the Cape Town Bergson, on account of the poet's having identified his mind and soul so completely with that of his subject. See *The Wayz-goose* (second page, with footnote).

"A clime so prosperous both to men and kine
That which were which a sage could scarce define."

Bull Hoek (pron. *hook*) *and Bondleswaart.* (1) Shooting raid on unarmed religious sect; (2) Bombing raid, by air, on a village which complained at a dog-tax.

THE FESTIVALS OF FLIGHT

Disselboom. Shaft of ox-wagon.

HORSES ON THE CAMARGUE

Camargue. Pampa at the mouth of the Rhone which together with the Sauvage and the desert Crau forms a vast grazing ground for thousands of wild cattle and horses. The Camarguais horses are a distinct race.

Trident. Dual allusion to the trident of Neptune and that carried by the guardians or cowboys of the Camargue.